WATER PLANET
Life in the
ARCTIC
OCEAN

Tamra B. Orr

PURPLE TOAD
PUBLISHING

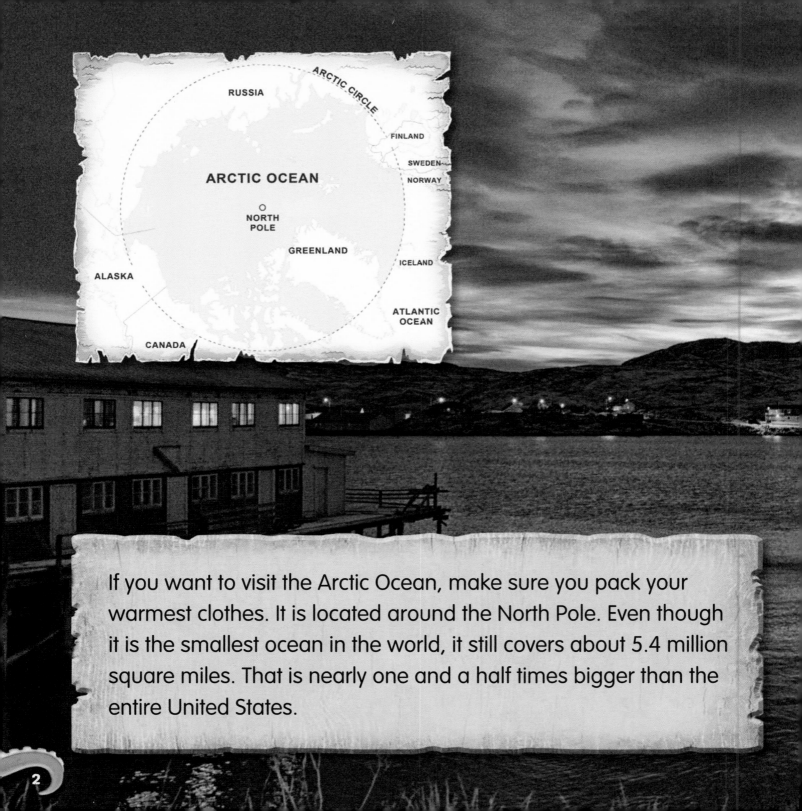

RUSSIA

ARCTIC CIRCLE

FINLAND

SWEDEN

NORWAY

ARCTIC OCEAN

NORTH POLE

GREENLAND

ICELAND

ALASKA

ATLANTIC OCEAN

CANADA

If you want to visit the Arctic Ocean, make sure you pack your warmest clothes. It is located around the North Pole. Even though it is the smallest ocean in the world, it still covers about 5.4 million square miles. That is nearly one and a half times bigger than the entire United States.

Despite the arctic cold, people make homes in many Norwegian villages like this one.

Many sea creatures eat plankton, plants or animals that drift along on the currents of the water.

The Arctic Ocean is landlocked. This means it is surrounded on every side by land. The deepest spot in this ocean is the Eurasian Basin **(yur-AY-zhun BAY-sin)**. It is 17,880 feet deep. You could stack up almost 1,000 adult male giraffes in it.

The Arctic Ocean has the least amount of salt of all the oceans. It is also incredibly cold. In the summer, the water may reach 32 degrees Fahrenheit **(FER-uh n-hahyt)**. During the winter, it is often way below zero! Brrrrr.

Polar cod have a kind of anti-freeze in their blood which keeps them from freezing in the cold waters.

A Polar bear walks on pack ice. All the wild polar bears in the world are found in the Arctic region. They spend more time in the water or on sea ice than they do on land. Their white coats help them hide in the world of snow and ice.

Parts of the Arctic Ocean stay frozen all year round. It has three types of ice. Polar ice never melts. It can be 6.5 feet thick in the summer. During the winter, it can be 164 feet thick.

At the edge of the polar ice is pack ice. It stays frozen only during the winter months. Ice that forms between the pack ice and land is called fast ice.

Bowhead whales are considered the longest living mammal in the world today. They can live over 200 years and are second in size only to the blue whale.

Beluga whale

A number of whales swim in the incredibly cold Arctic Ocean waters. The bowhead whale grows up to 60 feet long and weighs 100 tons. This is as much as five elephants! The bowhead has the largest mouth of any animal on earth. It swims along the ocean floor with its mouth open like a living vacuum cleaner to catch its prey.

The Arctic Ocean's white beluga whale is known as "the canary of the sea" because of the high-pitched calls it makes underwater. Its coloring helps it hide from polar bears and killer whales.

Many of the world's icebergs and glaciers are found in the Arctic Ocean. Glaciers **(GLEY-shers)** are large sheets of ice. They can spread out over miles. Icebergs are large pieces of glaciers that have broken off. They move through the water, pushed by water currents. Icebergs smaller than 16 feet across are often called growlers.

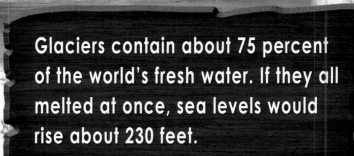

Glaciers contain about 75 percent of the world's fresh water. If they all melted at once, sea levels would rise about 230 feet.

The snow bunting is a small white bird that lives in the arctic. It runs on the ground and nests in cold rocks.

The narwhal (**NAR-wall**) is a whale that is known for its tusk, a long tooth that grows from its upper lip. This tooth is able to notice any changes in water temperature. It has earned the whale the nickname "unicorn of the sea." The narwhal can live up to 100 years and uses echolocation (**ek-oh-loh-KAY-shun**), or sound waves, to find its prey.

The narwhal is able to communicate by squealing, trilling, and clicking. The males sometimes use their tusks as a weapon in fighting with other males.

Walruses (**WALL-russ-es**) are huge marine mammals. Some grow as long as 11 feet and weigh up to 3,700 pounds. They have flippers, a wide head, small eyes, tusks, and whiskers. The tusks are used to cut through ice, in self-defense, and to help pull their body out of the water. Two-thirds of their lives are spent on the sea ice.

Walruses use their sensitive whiskers to find their food. They like to eat clams and mussels.

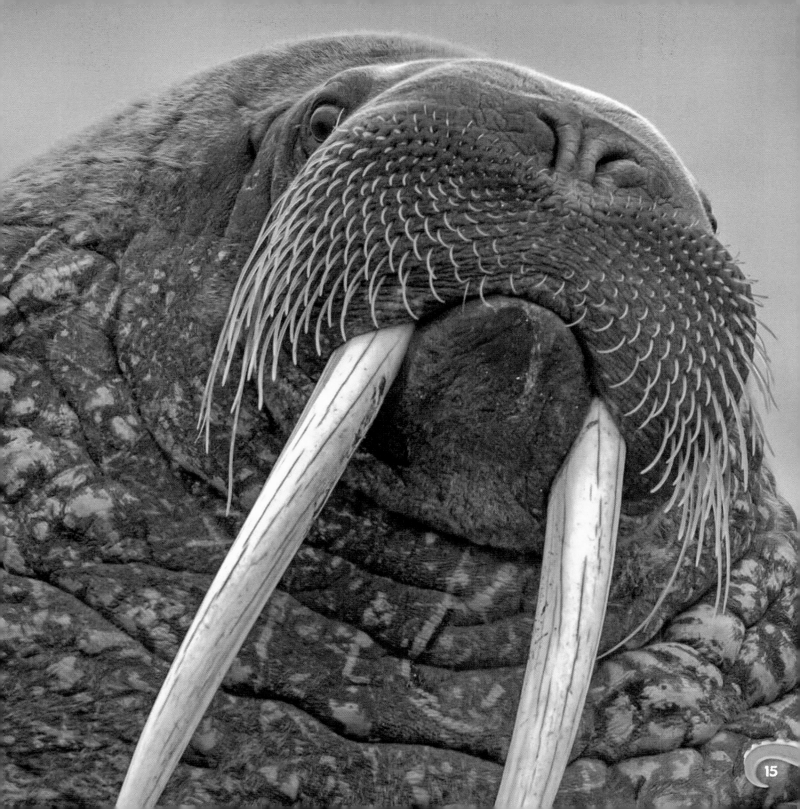

Sea spiders are not really insects, although they look like they are. They walk on the tips of their long, thin legs.

Living at the bottom of the Arctic Ocean is not easy. It is extremely cold and dark. Only a few creatures are able to survive there. Some sponges and worms do. Alien-looking sea spiders crawl along the ocean floor. The snow crab is also found there, although it is usually less than three inches long.

Snow crabs may be small, but they are considered a very tasty treat by humans.

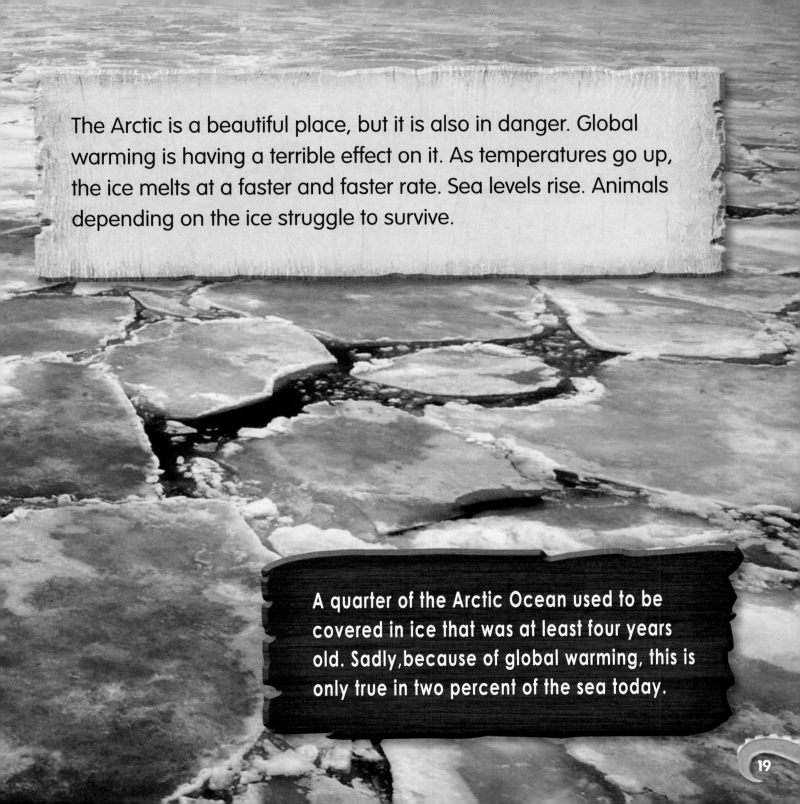

The Arctic is a beautiful place, but it is also in danger. Global warming is having a terrible effect on it. As temperatures go up, the ice melts at a faster and faster rate. Sea levels rise. Animals depending on the ice struggle to survive.

A quarter of the Arctic Ocean used to be covered in ice that was at least four years old. Sadly, because of global warming, this is only true in two percent of the sea today.

The Arctic Ocean is an amazing place. It is far more comfortable to study from a distance, however. It's too cold up close!

Polar bears travel on land and use sea ice to hunt for seals. The disappearance of that sea ice means danger for the bears.

FURTHER READING

Books

Gonzales, Doreen. *The Frigid Arctic Ocean*. Berkeley Heights, NJ: Enslow Elementary, 2013.

Green, Jen. *Arctic Ocean*. New York: Gareth Stevens Publishing, 2006.

Isaacs, Sally. *Helen Thayer's Arctic Adventure: A Woman and a Dog Walk to the North Pole*. Mankato, MN: Capstone Young Readers, 2016.

Oachs, Emily Rose. *Arctic Ocean*. Minneapolis, MN: Bellwether Media, 2016.

Spilsbury, Louise, and Richard Spilsbury. *Arctic Ocean*. Portsmouth, NH: Heinemann, 2015.

Woods, Michael. *Seven Natural Wonders of the Arctic, Antarctica, and the Oceans*. Minneapolis, MN: Twenty-First Century Books, 2009.

Web Sites

Defenders of Wildlife: "Basic Facts About the Arctic"
http://www.defenders.org/arctic/basic-facts-about-arctic

iTV.com: "Top 10 Facts You Need to Know about the Arctic"
http://www.itv.com/news/2013-04-10/top-10-facts-you-need-to-know-about-the-arctic/

National Geographic Kids: "Ten Facts about the Arctic"
http://www.ngkids.co.uk/places/ten-facts-about-the-arctic

basin (BAY-sin)—A natural bowl-shaped space that holds water.

current (KUR-rent)—An area of water that moves in one direction.

echolocation (EK-oh-loh-KAY-shun)—Finding objects by sending out sounds and determining the time for the echo to return.

glacier (GLAY-shur)—A huge, moving mass of ice formed from snow.

global warming (GLOW-bull WAR-ming)—The increase in earth's average temperatures causing changes in climate.

iceberg (Ahys burg)—A large, floating mass of ice broken off of a glacier.

landlocked (Land-lokd)—Shut in completely or almost completely by land.

plankton (PLANK-ton)—The very young form of many types of sea creatures; plankton is a major food source for many different animals.

prey (PRAY)—An animal hunted for food.

tusk (TUSK)—An extremely long tooth found in creatures such as elephants and walruses.

INDEX

Printing 1 2 3 4 5 6 7 8 9

ABOUT THE AUTHOR: Tamra Orr is the author of hundreds of books for readers of all ages. She loves the chance to learn about faraway lands and see what it is like to live there—all from the comfort of her work desk. Orr is a graduate of Ball State University, and is the mother of four. She lives in the Pacific Northwest and goes camping whenever she gets the chance.

Publisher's Cataloging-in-Publication Data
Orr, Tamra B.
  Arctic Ocean / written by Tamra B. Orr.
    p. cm.
Includes bibliographic references, glossary, and index.
ISBN 9781624693656
1. Arctic Ocean--Juvenile literature. I. Series: Water planet.
 GC401 2017
 551.468

eBook ISBN: 9781624693663

Library of Congress Control Number: 2017940567